Your Faith
CHRISTIANITY

By *Harriet Brundle*

You can find the **bold** words in this book in the Glossary on page 24.

PHOTO CREDITS

CONTENTS

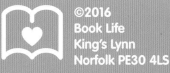

©2016
Book Life
King's Lynn
Norfolk PE30 4LS

ISBN: 978-1-910512-94-4

Written by:
Harriet Brundle

Designed by:
Drue Rintoul

A catalogue record for this book
is available from the British Library.

What is RELIGION?

Religion means to believe in or **worship** something, usually a god or gods. Many religions have important places, celebrate **festivals** and help people to live a good life.

There are lots of different religions. Some of the religions with the largest amount of followers are Christianity, Islam, Hinduism and Sikhism.

CHRISTIANITY

ISLAM

HINDUISM

SIKHISM

What is CHRISTIANITY?

Christianity is a religion that began over two thousand years ago. It is the largest religion in the world.

People who follow Christianity are called Christians and they believe in one god. Christians believe that God made the world and everything in it.

JESUS

Christians believe that Jesus is the son of God and that he was sent to Earth to spread God's word.

Christian people believe that Jesus was **crucified** and so the cross is an important symbol of the Christian faith.

Jesus came back to life on Easter Sunday. This is called the resurrection.

THE BIBLE

The Bible is a special book for Christians. The Bible is written in two parts, the Old Testament and the New Testament.

The Bible is a collection of writings by lots of different people. It was created over many hundreds of years. The Bible helps Christians to understand God and to live a good life.

Places of WORSHIP

The Christian place of worship is called a church. The outside of the church usually has a **steeple** with a cross on top, to remind us of Jesus.

Inside the church there are pews for people to sit on, so they can listen to the **vicar**. The vicar gives talks, called sermons, and reads from the Bible.

Vicar

Pulpit

13

Prayer in CHURCH

Christian people pray to show their love for God. They also pray to ask for God's help and forgiveness Praying can be done sitting, kneeling or standing.

When praying, some Christians choose to bow their heads
and put their hands together to show respect for God.
Prayer in a church can be led by the vicar or each person
can say their own prayers.

CHRISTENING

A young person is brought into Christianity when they are christened. Parents and Godparents make a promise to guide the child in their Christian faith.

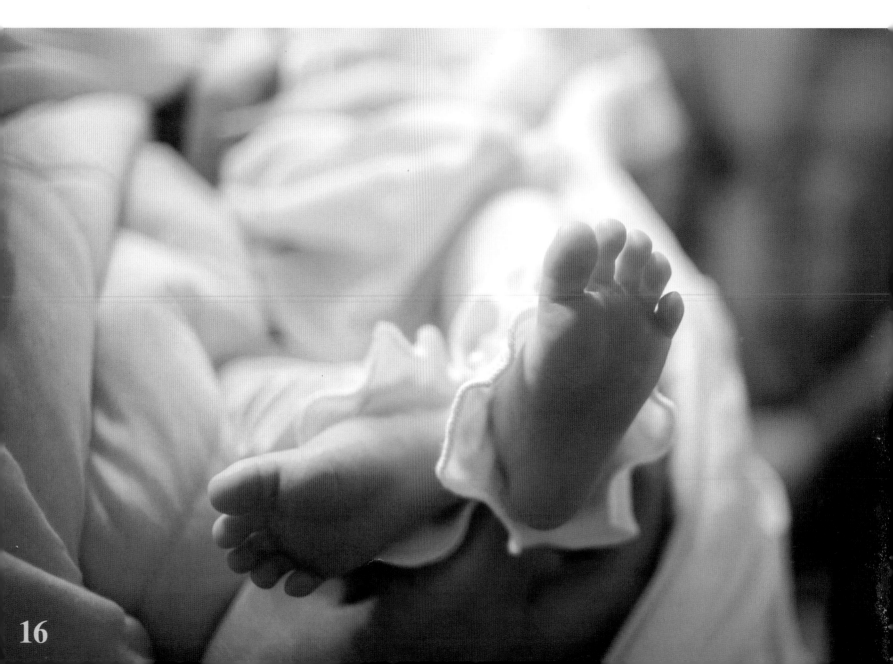

The vicar pours water over the head of the child and makes the sign of the cross. Family and friends come together to celebrate the christening.

When he or she is older, the child can make the promise for themselves. This is called confirmation.

MARRIAGE

A Christian marriage takes place in a church. The **ceremony** is performed by the vicar. **Hymns** are often sung and parts of the Bible are read out loud.

When two Christians get married, they stand before God and make promises to each other. They become husband and wife.

CHRISTIAN FESTIVALS

Christmas is a special time for Christians because it is when Jesus was born. Christian people exchange gifts and spend time with friends and family.

Easter is the most important Christian festival. On Good Friday, Christians remember Jesus being killed. On Easter Day, they celebrate his resurrection.

Easter eggs are a symbol of new life.

Facts about CHRISTIANITY

1 Christians believe Sunday is a special day. Sunday has **traditionally** been a day of worship for Christian people.

2 In the Bible, it says Jesus was able to walk on water.

3 The Bible contains Ten Commandments. These tell Christians how they should try to live, for example to have respect for your mother and father.

4 Smaller churches are called chapels. Very large churches are called cathedrals.

GLOSSARY

Ceremony a series of special acts that are performed on religious or social occasions

Crucified killed on a cross

Festivals when people come together to celebrate special events or times of the year

Hymns religious songs that are sung to God

Steeple the pointed part on top of a church

Traditionally ways of behaving that have been done over a long period of time

Vicar the person in charge of the church

Worship to show a feeling of respect

INDEX